# Chronicles of an ER/Forensic Nurse

Tammy Undiemi

Published by Tammy Undiemi, 2023.

CHRONICLES OF AN ER/FORENSIC NURSE

**First edition. April 13, 2023.**

Copyright © 2023 Tammy Undiemi.

ISBN: 979-8215108475

Written by Tammy Undiemi.

# Table of Contents

# Dedication

**Thank you**

Over the years, I did not realize how much my life as an ER / forensic nurse affected not only me but my family. I was a single mom for quite some time and told my children all of my horror stories hoping that I was giving them tools to recognize situations and how to get out of them safely, etc. In turn, I most likely made them afraid of the world. Before I grasped how much I had personally been affected, I was mostly emotionally absent, a skill I learned as a child. I kept everything bottled up for most of my life. I regret not being as emotionally connected and can only try to take what I have learned about myself and be better moving forward. So, to my daughters, I am sorry for that. I also thank you for being there for me even when it was tough for you.

In late 2011, I met my now husband. We met working in the same hospital. I realized later how incredibly helpful it was to not only have a partner in life, but someone who was actually involved with, and has seen the same things. Of course, not to the same extent, but at least he actually had an understanding of the things I was dealing with on a regular basis. I am certain he did not know what he was getting himself into, but he was there for me even when he didn't know what to say. To my husband, thank you for understanding even when you didn't have the details. Thank you for being supportive when many would have found it too heavy and left.

# Preface

Let me start with a little bit about myself so you can understand my frame of mind. I didn't have much guidance growing up and I was in no way sheltered from the real world. My dad was not part of my life by his own choice. I lived with my mom who struggled with drug addiction. Mostly she was single, but she did marry twice while I was growing up. One of those marriages would provide times that were somewhat normal, but the other was a living nightmare for all of us. There were 3 of us, my brother a year younger and my sister 3 years older. My sister kind of did her own thing but endured a lot so that my brother and I wouldn't have to. I mostly raised myself and my brother. I remember being alone for days at a time. I would go to the neighbors and ask for food to feed my brother. I stole jackets from the lost and found at school because he didn't have one. There were really bad and scary times and there were what I thought were normal or regular times. Looking back, most probably wouldn't agree that those things were normal or ok. I often think where was CPS when I was growing up? In hindsight, it was probably better not to be placed into the broken system that exists. I have no idea how we survived. I have no idea how I was never addicted to drugs. How am I not messed up? Somehow, I always felt protected and knew that the way we lived was wrong, and I would not choose that for my future.

As a teenager, I became angry. Looking for a way out, I was easily manipulated by an older man toward the end of high school and got married at 17. Immediately we had kids and I was miserable for 8 years. We divorced and once my youngest daughter was old enough for full-time preschool at 3, I went to nursing school. I felt so accomplished once I graduated and started working.

I was excited to work as a nurse in the ER. A little too confident in the beginning, but wanted to be good at my job and know that I did everything I could to save the life of my patients when it mattered. ER nurses are a different breed. There are many types of nurses and while there are commonalities, many do not thrive in an ER setting. I wanted to take every class and get every certification. Advanced life support and trauma certifications for both adults and children, and so many others. I had no idea what I was getting myself into when

I took a forensic nursing course. As a forensic nurse, you collect trace evidence from the human body (dead or alive), perform forensic photography, and testify as an expert witness. Sounds super cool huh? That's what I thought. Even with all I had been through as a child, I was not prepared for the things I would see, or more so what I cannot unsee.

# The Silence is Deafening

Let me explain what that means to me

Most people have no idea what's going on in their own backyard. Everyone assumes that if violent crimes are committed that they will hear about it on the local news. As a new nurse, I was shocked by the things I was seeing in the ER that no one seemed to know about. Your local fire department, EMS, police, and ER staff know, but why doesn't the news report it? I see and hear things on the news all the time but it's occasional and always in some other town or somewhere else. What about the crimes happening right here? By that, I mean everywhere. I have worked in many ERs across 4 different states, it's the same everywhere. I don't mean terrible injuries from car accidents or other trauma, etc. Those can be awful and life-changing, but I am talking about the ability of another person to physically take their hands and hurt another human in such intimate personal ways. It's not gunshot wounds or bar fights. It's the domestic violence, child abuse, trafficking, and sexual assaults that leave me without understanding. We have grown accustomed to those words, but the chronicles you are about to read will put them into a new perspective.

You can scrape someone off the highway and bring them to me in the ER. I will try to save their life. I don't lay awake at night and think about how bad the injuries were or how much their lives are derailed. What haunts me and keeps me from sleeping is what humans do to each other. Somewhere along the way, I determined that I needed to stop trying to understand why people do terrible things. I will never understand. The wires are crossed within the people who commit these crimes. Those who could never commit these crimes would never understand and shouldn't want to. I guess in a way I feel that if I were to understand, then does that make me just like them? Just as capable?

Think of the people in your neighborhood. One who is well-known and active in the community that you respect. Would you feel differently if you knew they physically abused their child, sexually assaulted someone, or beat up their partner? Trust me, these things are happening in your neighborhood too. What would you do if you found out that a neighbor had a secret room in their home and that trafficking victims were being held? I bet you are thinking that you pay too close attention or that your neighbors would never do that. You would know if people were in and out of a house nearby, right? That is what we all say.

Violent crime knows no boundaries. Anyone can be a victim and anyone can be a perpetrator. Rarely is it the scary stranger in the creepy van down the street. These people live next door, relate with neighbors, and are admired. The preacher, the teacher, the elderly, the young, the police officer, or the doctor. It's never whom you expect it to be and infrequently is it a stranger. The youngest victim I collected evidence from was 3 months old and the oldest 98. The youngest suspect I collected evidence from was 6 years old and the oldest 87.

Why do we hear so much unnecessary news but not the things we can do something about in our own communities? The silence screams from inside me. It is overwhelming. I want to shout it from the rooftops. Why aren't these things on blast?! I believe communities would be different and violent crime would be much less if the truth was revealed in real-time.

# Forensic Nursing Explained

Forensic nurses are specially trained to collect trace evidence from the human body of victims of violent crime. We are trained in forensic photography, work closely with law enforcement, and are considered expert witnesses in a court of law. These specially trained nurses can work in the medical examiner's office, hospital-based programs, and correctional facilities to name a few.

Forensic nursing is a unique skill set. I didn't realize it at first, but it was apparent just a few short years after getting the certification. Let me help you understand. In one of the states, I worked in, there were over 400,000 nurses and less than 350 nurses who held the same certifications as me. Of those 350, less than half with more than five years under their belt. Why? Why don't more nurses obtain this certification and help these victims? Is it because they can't handle it? I don't have an answer for that. One thing to consider is that the certification process is not easy to complete. I specialized in forensics for 13 years, have collected evidence from hundreds of victims, and certified more than 70 other nurses along the way.

Please note some details will be left out to protect the identity of victims and/ or suspects, law enforcement, or other nurses. Also, note that I may or may not have been the only nurse involved in the cases I discuss. I will tell each from my own perspective but may have been training with others, teaching, or consulting on cases that were not my own. Nevertheless, the stories remain the same.

# The Jason Mask Rapist

My scariest case

I was called into the ER very early one morning, 3 or 4 am after a young adult female checked in reporting sexual assault. She was pacing the room when I got there. She kept stopping and putting both her hands on the counter and looking around as if she can't process what was happening. She wasn't crying, she just kept repeating "I can't believe this."

She reported pulling into the apartment complex parking lot where her boyfriend lived. She got out of her car and a man approached her. She described him as very tall and broad. She states he was wearing a "Jason" mask. I knew she meant a hockey mask because I had seen the Jason movies before. She reported that he had a gun and instructed her to get back into the car. She followed instructions and got back into the car and so did he.

He made her drive to a secluded location and sexually assaulted her. She told me he had an accent, was "football player-type big" and uncircumcised. He then made her drive to an ATM and pull out as much money as she could. Once he got the money, he had her drive back to the same parking lot where he abducted her, she parked and he got out and left.

She was too scared to get out of her car so once he left, she waited for what she felt like was forever and then she drove straight to the hospital.

She was too scared to let me call the police at that moment. I should explain that in some states sexual assault is a mandatory law enforcement report, in others if the victim is over the age of 18 and under the age of 65, it is a choice. The victim has the right to choose whether to make a police report or not.

All states have the option of what is called an anonymous report. This means a victim can have evidence collected but not make a police report immediately. The evidence is stored for a specific period of time. If during that time the victim reports it to the police, then the evidence is processed. If no report is made within the timeframe, then the evidence is destroyed. In most states that timeframe is 2-5 years. People often have questions about this option. Why wouldn't someone want to make a report? Consider different situations. For example, a single mom who is assaulted by her boss. No family to help, and really feels like she is on her own. If she makes the report immediately, then obviously she has no job. If she has time to get out of the situation, then at least there is still some income while she is preparing.

Now, continuing the story. This patient was just in complete disbelief and wasn't sure what she wanted to do. So, I proceeded with evidence collection. I swabbed every part of her that needed to be swabbed, took pictures, and collected her clothes.

I discharged her with information about all the reporting options and tried to encourage her to make the report. I actually gave her my personal cell phone number. I still am not sure what compelled me to do that. Never before then, nor since, have I given my cell phone number to any victim.

A few days passed and I am almost done with a night shift when a college-age girl was brought to the ER by police. The police report that they responded to a car accident call and that when they arrived on the scene of the accident, the patient was crying and reported the following; She stated that she had been out with friends at a local bar and returned to her apartment. As she was getting out of her car, a man approached wearing a hockey mask and carrying a gun. He made her get back into the car and told her to drive. While she was driving, she purposefully wrecked her car into another car. She knew that those people would have to get out of their car and maybe could help her. When she hit the other car, the masked man jumped out of her car and ran, somehow leaving behind a shoe.

I knew immediately this was the same guy. I told the police officers that I couldn't tell them specifics but that there was another case within the last 48 hours from a different jurisdiction that was the exact same scenario. Same description of the perp down to the accent, the size, and the hockey mask. They listened and immediately had her car processed for evidence.

Luckily, this victim wasn't sexually assaulted. She told me he whispered in her ear "Get back in the car.". I swabbed her ear because I know that DNA can be transferred from breath or saliva very easily. It is easy and cheaper for the crime lab to process and it stays on the skin for days. Yes, I said days. Most people think that if a person has showered or it's been a few days that all evidence is lost. Not true. Technology is amazing. Every state has a different protocol but most will collect evidence up to 5 days after the assault, even if the patient has had showers, etc.

Have you ever felt the breath of a person who is whispering or talking to you? I can't stand it when people do this because I know their DNA is there and I can't wash it off. It completely grosses me out!

It was a long night/morning and I was tired, but I went home after this and took my girls to school. My plan was to lay down just for a few hours and then get moving for the day. Just as my head hit the pillow, I got a phone call. It's her, the first victim.

She is sitting in the parking lot of the local police department. She says she wants to make a report, but she is scared. I knew one of the detectives who was a female. I felt like she might be more comfortable with a female. I told her to wait and not leave and that I would have someone come out to her.

Here I am calling the local police department trying to get through their damn automated system in a hurry. That works out well, right? Ugh! Can't I just push zero and talk to someone? Don't try that if you are in a hurry, you end up starting the entire call all over.

Finally, I get to someone in the sex crimes division. I ask for the female detective and give her a quick version of the story and tell her the victim is waiting outside in her car. I also make sure she understands that I have another victim who escaped the same suspect but it's a different jurisdiction.

For those of you who don't know, jurisdictions don't talk to each other unless there is a reason to. One jurisdiction may not know about a current case that fits that same MO in a nearby jurisdiction, etc.

THEY WOULD IF IT WAS REPORTED ON THE LOCAL NEWS!!

Just saying.

Fast forward. There are eight victims across multiple jurisdictions in 12 weeks. All with the same description, the same MO. Big guy with a gun, wearing a hockey mask, and approaches women in parking lot as they get out of their cars. Makes them get back in their car and drive somewhere, assaults them, and makes them go to an ATM to withdraw money. All describe his accent, uncircumcised penis, very tall with broad shoulders, and very scary.

The local jurisdictions collaborated and put two plain clothes police officers in unmarked cars in every apartment complex parking lot across the city.

Finally, they got him! An adult male fitting the description to a T was found sitting in his car in the parking lot at a local apartment complex. They check his ID, and run his plates, but guess what? They have no legal grounds to hold him or even take him in for questioning. The law prevents this without probable cause, blah, blah, blah. Why can't they at least question him?

At least now they have a potential suspect.

The police apply for and obtain a search warrant. Guess who this guy is? He is a 19-year-old (Yes, I said 19) active-duty soldier who is stationed nearby and about to be deployed for the first time. They search his barracks and find a duffle bag with the gun, the hockey mask, and other items that were identified by the victims. They also found a single shoe that is a perfect match to the one left behind in the car of the victim who got away.

I get yet another call in the middle of the night, 2am. It's the Police stating "we have a suspect we need evidence collected on." My heart sank because I knew who it was, it had to be. I said okay, and hung up the phone. Inside I panicked because I had listened to the stories of each of his victims. I knew how terrifying he was. Did the hockey mask make it more frightening because of the Jason movies? I'm not sure, I just know that I was scared to.

When a suspect is brought in for evidence collection, they either have to consent or a warrant must be issued. Suspects are always escorted by police. So, I knew I wouldn't be alone with him, but I was still scared. By the time I got to the hospital, I had put my game face on. I was trying not to throw up but acted like a boss.

Since the last assault had occurred within the timeframe for evidence collection, I had to swab his penis, scrotum, mouth, and take his blood. I had to pluck his pubic hair. Imagine that. Knowing the person in front of you has sexually assaulted 12 people in the last 2 months. As he sat there in shackles, he stared a hole through me. He was glued to my every move. I couldn't help but wonder what he is thinking about me. Was he enjoying this? Is he trying to memorize what I look like? What is he thinking? At this point, I wish I had a mask.

Boy were these victims right. He was huge. 6'6" tall and so broad he took up the entire doorway. All I could see are visions of this guy in a hockey mask and think how petrified I would be if I were in a parking lot and he approached me. What would I do, how would I react? Truth is, I don't know. I think to myself, if anyone ever pulls a gun on me and tells me to get in my car, I would say no. Just take the chance of them shooting me right there because I can't fathom the thought that I would be tortured for 2 days and then killed. Just shoot me, I'm not getting in that car. But could I think that quickly? I don't know.

At least now we can rest a little easier because he had been caught. His DNA was run through the CODIS (Combined DNA Index System) database and matched to 5 unsolved sexual assaults in his hometown. The first offense was committed when he was 16. Wow.

He was tried in each jurisdiction separately, then court-martialed and sent to prison for life. I had to testify in each case. Even years later, I would receive subpoenas to testify in the unsolved cases of his hometown. Here I am following this guy from county to county, state to state testifying against him. Does he connect me with the reason he was convicted? Should I be afraid?

A few crazy details from the trials: The parking lot of the apartment complex where he was first identified by those two plain clothes officers, was the same complex where the girl that wrecked on purpose lived and was taken from. He had gone back for her.

The very first victim, if you remember, she was going to see her boyfriend. He testified that he was watching for her through the window. He saw "a very large guy" approach her and watched them leave. He stated he saw the mask, but that he wasn't sure what was going on and he was waiting for her to come back and fell asleep. Wait, what? You were waiting for your girlfriend, saw her drive up and get out of her car. You watched a large man in a mask approach her and they leave and you do nothing?!?! To this day, I am astonished by how much people do not trust their own eyes, their gut. They don't believe what they are seeing and just wait instead of trying to intervene and help each other.

All the video from the ATMs were shown in court. Picture this, each victim leans forward to put their ATM card in the machine and behind them in the passenger seat, you see a large person in a hockey mask. It was like watching a horror film in court.

So scary.

# 4-year-old Girl, No Disclosure

Why did she lie?

Before I tell you about this next case, you should know some basic forensic facts about females.

First, all females have a hymen. It doesn't ever go away, it does change with puberty but it doesn't matter if you are 8 or 80, it's still there. I promise.

I am not sure why men think this, but women cannot see inside their own vaginas. Seriously, we can't.

No, semen cannot be seen with the naked eye. It does not glow, nor does it do cartwheels. All bodily fluid can look the same (especially if its dry) to the naked eye. Only testing in a lab can determine what is what. I have had police officers ask me "did you see semen during the exam?" Uhm, no. Just no. I was standing next to a doctor once who asked a patient "Did you see semen in your vagina" OMG. genius. (This is where I insert the forehead slap emoji.)

There is no way to "look and tell" if anything has happened. Most cases of assault do not result in injury, even in children. On the other hand, you could have injury with consensual sex. No matter the age, we can't "Look and tell". If a child has not started puberty yet, we can do exams outside the timeframe of evidence collection to look for healed trauma but not to collect evidence looking for DNA. Again, only if they have not hit puberty.

Finally, parents cannot force a minor to have an exam. If I had a dollar for every time someone brought their kid in and asked for an exam "to see if they are still a virgin" I would be rich. I have had parents bring their preteens/teens in after they snuck out and got caught. The parents say "I am not sure what he/she was doing, I want this done so we know if they were having sex or not." It doesn't work like that. As I mentioned, I cannot look and tell. Also, the patient has to consent to the exam, if they say nothing happened or that they don't want it. I can't do it. It doesn't matter if the parent says "He/She is a minor and I'm the parent." A forensic exam is not like a flu shot. I can hold your kid down to give them a flu shot, but I cannot force someone to have a forensic exam unless there is a warrant. That would be considered sexual assault in its own way. All evidence that is collected has to go to the crime lab for processing. I can't collect and keep it, and the crime lab won't spend money and time processing samples just to see if someone has had sex. They are busy trying to process evidence for crimes. Come on people.

*The story.*

The Aunt of a 4-year-old brought her niece in. The Aunt is her legal guardian and has stated "I just know something is happening to her". When asked what that meant, she couldn't answer. The child had not made any statements or drawn any inappropriate pictures, etc. Why did her aunt think this? Children are sometimes hard to figure out. They are not always forthcoming. The little girl denied that anyone had ever touched her. As a forensic nurse, I knew that this didn't necessarily mean that nothing happened. We did move forward and complete the exam which was normal. No signs of new injury, no signs of old injury.

Of course, CPS and Law Enforcement were notified. We referred the little girl to the child advocacy center where a forensic psychologist can interview her. No disclosures are made. Which means she never admitted that anyone had done anything to her.

Several weeks later, her aunt brought her in again. Same complaint. "I just know someone is messing with her." Patient, again, denies every question and again has a normal genital exam. This time all pictures are sent to another forensic nurse to be sure I wasn't missing anything. Healed trauma can be hard to spot. That nurse was in agreeance, normal.

This time a few months go by and in walks the aunt AGAIN. Same statements. Ok. It's time to take a closer look at the aunt. Are you mentally stable? Why does she keep making these accusations? She only keeps repeating that it's a gut feeling and that she doesn't know how to help her niece. I honestly felt bad for this woman but what can I do? The exam is negative x 3, the forensic psychologist hadn't gotten any disclosure out of this kid after multiple visits. Are we missing something? A visit to the house from CPS is unfounded. All appears normal.

A few months go by and the next thing I know the police are bringing this little girl back to me. Wait, what? Turns out that the adult male that lived next door to the little girl was arrested in a child pornography sting operation. After seizing his computer and all child pornography from the home, they found multiple pictures of this little girl fully penetrated by him.

Boom. (Insert mind blown emoji here.)

In training, we are taught that penetration most often does NOT result in injury but it is hard to think that if an adult male fully penetrates a small child that there is no indication on exam. How on earth does little girls vagina look normal?!?! Did I miss something? During all forensic exams a high-power camera is used with magnification to ensure we see even micro tears that are not visible with the naked eye. The cameras we use are incredible. To put it into perspective, on adults, I can even get clear pictures of a cervix which is high inside the vaginal vault. The pictures in this case were reviewed by more than one person to ensure quality and agreement, etc. All involved agreed that the vaginal exam is normal.

Why didn't this little girl answer the questions honestly? How does she know what to lie about? Forensic psychologists use techniques to trick children to get the truth, how did she avoid this? She is 4.

Auntie was right. Listen to your gut people. Could we have done anything differently in this situation? I am not sure. We didn't discount the aunt's statements. We did exams every time, they were just normal. How did the neighbor have enough access to her that there was time for this to take place?

So many questions. This situation just reinforced what we learned in training. There is no way to look and tell if something happened or not. There is not always injury. The human body is very forgiving and most children are assaulted by people they know. These people groom them little by little to try and avoid injury. If they cause injury someone will see it and start asking questions.

# 11-year-old Prostitute

She just wants to be loved

Mid-morning on a weekday, police bring in an 11-year-old female. She was discovered pimping herself out on craigslist at a local mall. Someone at the mall had watched her walk across the street with an older man and then back into the mall with a different man. After witnessing this a few times, the employee called police reporting "it just didn't seem right." (Finally, someone listened to their gut!)

When approached by police, her phone was confiscated. It had her craigslist page pulled up, and transcripts from four "johns" from that morning that she had hooked up with, were easily found. Believe me, there were more in line. She would have them meet her at a specific place near the mall, then take her into the mall and purchase things she wanted before going across the street to a hotel where she would have sex with them. She was in possession of purses, clothes, an additional phone, and makeup that the johns collectively purchased for her.

When I entered the room, she was wearing a dress that was way too big and very inappropriate for her age. She had on a pair of heels that didn't even fit her. Imagine an 11-year-old wearing 4-inch heels that are at least 3 sizes too big. You could see that there were at least two inches of empty space at the back of the shoe. I had this thought in my head that she looked like she was playing dress-up. As I talk to her, she is answering questions like it's just a conversation. She is not upset or embarrassed. She isn't scared or mad. Just normal conversation. I collected the clothes that she is wearing, plus all the clothes that the johns purchased for her. I felt bad taking them, but they were considered evidence. The dumb johns made all purchases with credit cards. Don't get me wrong, I'm glad they are dumb because that and the craigslist accounts are how we can convict them. Undeniable proof. What world do they live in that they are totally comfortable using credit cards that connect each item purchased to them? They didn't even try to hide it. Not even plausible deniability. Oh, and Craigslist? I mean you might as well jump up and down with a sign that says I am a pedophile!

Based on the events she described that day, I collect swabs from her mouth, chest, breast, vagina, anus, and random places on her body. Throughout all of this, she was telling me her story. This girl was living with her mother until 2 months prior when her mom was killed by her own pimp.

She was then sent to live with her grandmother who didn't want her. She told me that she had two reasons for pimping herself out. One was to earn money and the other to hopefully become pregnant from someone that day.

Excuse me? What?

Yep, I said she was trying to get pregnant. When I asked her why, her response word for word was "I was just hoping that if I have a baby, I can love them and then they will love me back."

Think of any 11-year-old girl that you know. Imagine sitting there listening to her say these things to you. What would your response be? Do you think you can help her understand the magnitude of the situation?

I struggled to find the words to respond. All she wanted was someone to love her. I told her that I bet her mother loved her and wanted more for her than the life she was leading.

In these situations, we don't test for STDs because it would be too soon to detect. We treat as though there was an exposure to all of them hoping to prevent development. We also give Plan B or "the morning-after pill" to prevent pregnancy. The patient told me that she would take the antibiotics as long as I promised her none of them would harm a baby just in case she was pregnant from that day and she absolutely refused the pregnancy prevention medication.

There were two other nurses helping care for this kiddo. One I was training to collect evidence and one just doing regular hospital stuff. The patient was given all the medication. There may or may not have been a morning-after pill mixed in with all the antibiotics. There may or may not have been a medication error. I wasn't in the room, so I really don't know for sure. Someone had to do (or maybe didn't do) the right thing for this kid.

Her grandmother showed up but expressed that she didn't want her. Even if you didn't want your grandchild, wouldn't you be embarrassed or have some reservations admitting it? Not this chick, blunt and direct, "I don't want her." How can you look a child in the eye and say something so hurtful? No wonder why the little girl's own mother was so lost. Look at who her mother was.

This poor girl. CPS was involved and told the grandmother that she was the legal guardian, and if she wanted to give her up for adoption, she would have to do it the right way and could not "abandon" her in the ER. If she chose to not take her home, the grandmother would be charged with abandonment. One of the hardest things I've ever done is let that little girl leave with her grandmother.

I often think of her and wonder what happened to her. Was she miserable with her grandmother, adopted, or is she still a prostitute because that's all she knows?

# 5-month-old Female Capital Murder Case

I didn't want to save her

Full disclosure, this case disturbed me enough to make me take a break from forensics for two weeks. That may not seem like much, but this was the only break I ever took in all my years of this job.

I was the charge nurse in the ER, midday one day EMS calls with a 5-month-old female CPR in progress. We spring into action to get ready for what we call "a code". We get the right people, the right equipment, and medication as we wait for their arrival. EMS rolls in and they are still doing compressions. We take over and follow our normal protocol for resuscitation. EMS reported that the parents were getting ready for work and that the baby was in a bouncer type baby seat in the living room and was strapped in. One of them claimed to have found the 3-year-old sister sitting on top of the baby when they came in and that the baby wasn't breathing.

After a few rounds of medications and CPR, we got her heartbeat back. One of the first things we do in this situation no matter the age is get a rectal temperature. Body temp is very important and can make a huge difference in treatment and recovery.

That is when I discover that there is more to the story. This baby has been anally penetrated and I know it immediately. As she stabilizes, I began to meticulously examine her body. There are other injuries in different stages of healing. There was a scabbed over area, what I would find out later was a cigarette burn to the top of her head. Her left thumb was badly bruised and swollen. There were bruises on each side of her lower abdomen, and bruising noted to her lower spine. Cuts and abrasions underneath her chin and to her chest. Both of her knees look like they are skinned. Strange because she wasn't crawling yet at 5 months old. I took tons of pictures. I swabbed her anus and vagina and collected the clothes and diaper she had on.

She codes again. (Her heart stops)

All I can think is, I don't want to save her. I didn't want her to live. I was screaming inside. What is wrong with me? Who doesn't want a baby to live? ME! I did not want her to live, she had suffered enough! What kind of life would she have?

We got her back. (Her heart started beating again) She was flown out to a pediatric ICU.

I walked around on auto pilot getting things together, making sure everyone else was ok. Of course, the entire team is upset. Even when it isn't something horrible like this, coding a child is always tough to handle. Then I sat down by myself and I cried. I then had to catalog all the evidence and look through all the photographs so I could log them and document my findings from each one.

As I looked through the pictures, the images of this baby were flashing through my mind. The details are burned into my memory. These images would haunt me for years to come. I cannot tell you the number of nights insomnia persists and the images of many victims flash through my mind one by one, over and over.

Her feet were so white that they almost looked fake. To this day, I can describe every photo in detail. As I was going through the magnified images, I note the small round bruises along the lower spine. There are bruises on each side of the lower abdomen more linear. That was when I recognize these are all finger prints. The linear bruises on each side of the abdomen were thumb prints and the smaller round ones along her lower spine were from the fingertips of the perpetrator. I know immediately this is how he was holding her while penetrating her. Encircling her body, thumbs anchored on each side of the lower abdomen and hands wrapped around her with the fingertips settling on the lower spine. I had this vision in my head of her screaming during this assault. What kind of monster could do this? I stop before navigating through the other pictures. I just couldn't bear to look at them.

The parents never made it to the ER because they were being questioned on scene by the police. The police officer that was present in the ER was informed of the initial suspicion and advised that if any other children are in the home, that they would need a forensic exam as well.

It took me the rest of my shift to document the injuries, catalog the evidence and photos.

There were many tears at home that night. Thank God my husband not only works in the medical field, but actually the same hospital and in the ER. He was there, so he knows. He kind of gets it. He doesn't see all the details of the things I see, but often he has at least been in the room or he sees enough to know what monsters humans can be.

After incidents like this, most hospitals hold what is called a critical stress debriefing. This takes place within 24 hours of the situation and everyone involved is brought together where the incident is talked about. At the end, you leave it in the room and move forward. So, the next day, our leadership gathered everyone involved to talk about this case. I was not ready. It was too raw. So, I decided, I'm wasn't going. My husband knew this without even asking. He came to the ER and asked me to go get coffee. I agreed. When I walked into the coffee shop at the hospital, everyone is there. We all sort of shuffled walking toward the hospital chapel. I was overwhelmed and wanted to run, but didn't know how I should react. It took everything I had to put one foot in front of the other.

In the chapel, a few different people speak. I couldn't say a word because I was trying not to lose it and I mean really lose it. There are tears rolling down my face but I know there is a lot more emotion that I just can't bear to face. I couldn't let it out. I couldn't find words that even describe what I saw, or what I know. No one in that room knows what position she was held in while she was assaulted, or that the bruises on her spine and her abdomen are actually fingerprints. No one in that room knows that the abrasions on her knees go in both directions and that 5-month-old babies don't get skinned knees. No one in that room had to take and look through all those pictures. Yes, they saw her, helped save her, but they don't know what I know. Most did not see that her anus was just sitting open. The sphincter that normally closes the anus tightly had been torn.

I didn't say a word the entire time. I listened to others talk but was not really thinking about what they said. I was distracted by the flashing images in my head. I heard the chaplain ask my husband a question and though I don't remember the question, I remember his answer. He stated "Well, it's hard. There are lots of tears at home and I don't know what to say." Shit. This is affecting not just me, but my family. What about my girls? What do they think? Have I been selfish all these years and not paid attention to how this affects them?

Over the years many have asked me why and how I keep doing this. I had never found a way to put into words how I felt and why I kept going. Until that day. At the end of the critical stress debriefing, the chaplain said; "If we have to endure being touched by this evil every day to save another child, then we will keep doing it." I would repeat that sentence to myself many times over the years. I guess I felt a professional obligation to keep going because I now knew it was a unique skill set.

The baby died the next day. Her cause of death was a perforated bowel. Living tissue looks very different than dead tissue. The medical examiner is unable to prove sexual assault but the evidence I collected and the pictures I took prove sexual assault and put capital murder on the table. This means the death penalty. The perpetrator was mom's boyfriend. I testified against him and had to show the jury each piece of evidence, each picture, and explain all of it. It was a slam dunk for the prosecuting DA. He was found guilty and now we go to the sentencing part of the trial. He was given the death penalty. I know this seems crazy, but it kind of messed with my head a little bit. The evidence I collected sentenced this guy to death.

I know he made his own decisions and a jury of his peers found him guilty. The law chose his punishment, but it still messes with my head on a different level. I know he didn't die because of me, but he kind of did....

# Unidentified Adult Female

Who is she? Who did this?

I was working in the ER on a weekend and early one morning we received a radio transmission from a helicopter. They were transporting an unidentified adult female who had been found naked laying on the side of the road in the middle of nowhere. She was barely alive, intubated (on life support), and unstable.

We stabilize her. She has been severely beaten, from head to toe. I slowly looked over every inch of her body. I began taking pictures, swabbing everything, used a UV light to see if there was anything detectable on her skin, etc.

She had circumferential bruising around both wrists and ankles. This indicated she had been bound by something. One of her breasts had been almost completely cut off. I could tell that a serrated knife was used to do this. Her vagina had been severely burned, both inside and out. $2^{nd}$ and $3^{rd}$ degree burns. How in the world do you burn the inside of someone's vagina? Can you imagine the pain? This woman had been tortured. I imagined being her and someone cutting my breast away from my body. I imagined being burned in the same manner. How she must have prayed to just die or at least be knocked out. Something, anything, to just not feel the agony it must have been.

This is the first time in my forensic career I collected teeth as evidence. She had been hit so hard that it knocked out some of her teeth. One of which was tangled in her hair. I brushed the leaves and vegetation out of her hair onto a folded piece of paper and sealed them in an envelope. I have to work quickly as the patient needs to go to the operating room. Her breast would have to be removed and the burns she sustained had closed off her urethra which is just inside the vaginal vault. She would have to have her urethra fixed to drain urine. I went to the OR still collecting evidence and heard the surgeons discussing how to repair the damage. The surgeon actually had to create a urethra that exited through her belly button. She would need a catheter for the rest of her life just to pee.

After the surgery and evidence collection were complete, the victim was moved to ICU. Since no one knew where the offense was committed there was no jurisdiction that wanted to take responsibility. The US Marshalls had to take the case. They came into the hospital to get her fingerprints to try and identify her. They took custody of the evidence.

The victim spent approximately one week on life support. She finally did wake up and was so scared that she would not give up the name of the person who did this to her. She was taken into the witness protection program and I do not know the outcome of this case. I don't know if the person.....animal responsible ever spent a day in jail, or if he would be allowed to torture someone else in the future.

She did answer some questions. The burns were from a curling iron that was placed in her vagina by this man. She reports that she thought he was going to assault her with it but then she heard him plug it in. She watched him turn it on and says he just sat there grinning as it was heating up burning her slowly from the inside. He was naked and pleasuring himself as he watched her scream in agony. She also stated that he had actually used a steak knife to try and remove her breast.

I struggled with this one too. It is hard to describe how intentional, intimate, and horrific her injuries were. How long did he have her? Did she know him? I have prayed many nights that this kind of torture is not inflicted on anyone else, ever.

Would it be wrong to wish the perpetrator receive the same torment that he inflicted, or would that make me like him?

# College Age Female

My first case as a forensic nurse

I was working in the ER over the weekend and early in the morning, a college-age female checked in reporting sexual assault. She reported waking in the apartment of a coworker whom she has recently filed a sexual harassment complaint against at their place of employment. She remembers nothing. She woke up without her clothes on and was hysterical.

She stated there was a birthday party for a different coworker at a local bar. Many attended and as college kids indulge, there were many drinks involved. She remembers going to the bar and drinking, but does not remember leaving the bar or anything until waking.

I collected trace evidence from her body that morning, including swabs from inside her mouth, outside and inside her vagina and rectum. I took vials of blood and urine, & performed forensic photography. I switched on a UV light and turned off the lights to see if there are other indications of bodily fluids on her skin that I should swab. I collected all of the clothes she had on including her shoes.

We give clothes to these patients to wear home since their clothes are taken as evidence. Processing at the crime lab will destroy them and most don't want them back anyway.

The police were called and came to take her statement. Guess what the first questions where from the police officer? "Well, how much did you have to drink? Are you sure you didn't consent and just don't remember?" What should the patient say? She truly didn't remember.

I felt bad for her. I could see this internal battle. She was asking herself "Was I assaulted?" "Does the fact that I was so drunk excuse the fact that I was passed out and unable to consent?" "If he was sober, doesn't that make it a crime?" "Is it my fault?"

These investigations take several months. Many months later I received a subpoena to testify in a jury trial. Believe you me, I was freaking out! I was going to testify in a jury trial as an expert witness in the first case I ever collected evidence on. I asked myself, "Am I an expert?" I surely did not feel like one.

It is at the trial where I hear the whole story.

A friend that attended the same party reported that at the night's end, the college-age female was highly intoxicated. She was outside on the sidewalk with everyone else and called her boyfriend to pick her up. She wasn't sure exactly which bar she was at, so she handed her phone to the girl who was standing next to her and says "Tell him where I am so he can come get me". This girl she handed her phone to didn't know either, and then hands the phone to another...

Guess who that was? Yep, the coworker who has been accused of sexual harassment. He hung up the call and stated he will be happy to take her home as he had not had much to drink and knows where she lives. Her coworkers agree as they did not know about the pending sexual harassment complaint or any other details. Now, don't judge. Her close friends knew, but not other coworkers. The video feed from the bar that night showed that the female is clearly intoxicated and needed help even walking and getting into his car. Which he provided.

The video feed from the apartment complex where the suspect lived showed him lifting her out of the car. It showed him put his shoulder under her arm and drape one of her arms across his shoulders. He griped that wrist with one hand and placed his other arm behind her and sort of gripping her at the waist to hold her up. The video showed her head hanging down in front of her and barely bobbing. She was not walking. Her feet were dragging, toes down behind her as he was taking her into his apartment. At one point there is a shot of her face and she was clearly not even conscious.

The victim testified that she has no memory and reports to the jury how she woke up. She talked about the harassment that took place where they were employed; and stated that the suspect continued to text her even after that night. She wasn't sure how to respond and tried to be neutral before eventually just blocking his number.

The jury watched the videos from outside the bar, and from the suspect's apartment. They were informed about the harassment at work, and listened to the testimony from the girl at the party. After a short deliberation, the suspect was found not guilty. NOT GUILTY.

The jury stated that they didn't feel like someone who was a victim of sexual assault would respond to a text message from the perpetrator. That's it. What?! I couldn't believe it.

I learned two very important things from this trial. The first; is that we as humans are bad at recognizing the fact that we are victims. It is too often that we try to justify events. "If I wouldn't have been drinking" or "If I wouldn't have been there". We blame ourselves. It's different if someone shoots or stabs you. That is a no-brainer. But think about workplace violence or this situation. Would you immediately consider yourself a victim? Would you have questioned yourself?

The second thing I learned from this trial, is that we all react to every situation in an individual way.

What do you think of when you think of a victim of violent crime? I feel like most people (including the jury in this case) have this picture in their heads of a woman or child cowering in the corner, crying, and afraid. That is what you see in the movies and on TV. This is the furthest from the truth. Most people go through many emotions just in the time frame that I am with them.

Think of a minor fender bender. We all react differently to those types of things. Some people are really upset and crying, it's the end of the world. Some are angry, screaming, and placing blame. Others are totally chill, just waiting to make a police report and all is fine in the world.

I suppose it depends on life experience and coping mechanisms. Moving forward, I promised myself I would make sure to teach the jury these two things in every trial that I testified in.

# 3-Month-old Baby Boy

My youngest victim

I was called into the ER for a 3-month-old baby who was brought in by police after someone witnessed his mother throw his little body across a room and into the wall at a local hotel. It was my job to take pictures and document any bruising or other injuries, as well as collect trace evidence if there was a potential for it to be there.

For children that are victims of suspected abuse, we do what is called a skeletal survey. Basically, it's a full body x-ray to see if there is evidence of old or if there are new fractures. The skeletal survey showed a forearm fracture of both bones. This is hard to accomplish in a 3-month-old. Their bones are pliable if you will. Very hard to break. Think about the size of bones in the forearm of a 3-month-old. That's like trying to break a 3–5-inch piece of solid wood with your fingers. It isn't easy to do. You might see one of those bones with a break if someone picked them up by one arm, or the family dog stepped on it, etc. But both bones in the exact same place? The only thing I could determine is that someone physically took his little arm and intentionally tried to break it.

What would make someone want to try to break this baby's arm?

I meticulously looked this poor baby over, head to toe. As I got to his tiny little bottom, I saw a small, sort of scratching patterned abrasion leading into his anus. They weren't deep, but perfectly and evenly spaced. There was a small tear in the surrounding anal tissue as well. I could tell he has been sodomized. What object could have caused those marks? I couldn't think of anything. Speaking with the officers and showing them the pictures, they couldn't figure it out either.

This poor little guy was admitted to the hospital, mom was arrested. Of course, CPS (Child Protective Services) was notified.

Police officers that responded to the initial call, collected everything they found at the scene. This was proven beneficial as a toothbrush found on the scene was found to have fecal matter belonging to the baby on it. He was sodomized with a toothbrush by his mother. This explains the evenly spaced scratch pattern leading into his anus.

The charges were elevated to include felony child abuse and aggravated sodomy.

It was later discovered that mom had been convicted of child abuse in another state and had a 2-year-old removed from her custody and all parental rights terminated. She came across state lines to have this baby so it wouldn't be taken from her.

How is it that a person convicted of child abuse can cross state lines and go undetected? It's not like she was using another name. She was receiving state assistance for health insurance. Why doesn't the system flag those who have been convicted of violent crimes when they apply for government assistance? This way when they cross state lines and apply, the current state/government services departments are alerted of the history. We could have saved this kid from going through any of it.

I know, criminals have rights too. I don't want to hear it. If you commit a violent crime, you deserve the consequences. Flagging her wouldn't necessarily prevent her from getting help, but since it was for pregnancy, it would have put the baby on CPS radar to check on, etc.

We give criminals too much freedom in this country.

# Attempted Murder by Strangulation

Worst <u>nonfatal</u> strangulation case

Towards the end of a busy shift in the ER on a weekday, I received notification that a patient checked in reporting sexual assault. I was training another ER nurse to collect evidence, and so we go in together. The first thing I noticed is her eyes. Without her saying a word, I knew she had been strangled. The small capillaries in her eyes are ruptured so the white parts of her eyes were bloody. There were small pinpoint purple dots on her face. These were also from microscopic blood vessels that ruptured from the pressure of being strangled. Basically, the blood comes to the surface.

She reported that 6 months ago she filed for divorce from an abusive husband. She stated it was a nasty divorce and he had been arrested for domestic violence. There was a temporary restraining order for 3 months that was now expired. She stated they had actually had a few normal, civil conversations in the past several weeks as they had children and mutual friends.

She finally felt safe enough to get some items that were given to her in the divorce decree but she had previously left at their old house because she was afraid. She reported driving to his house with her two small dogs. She knocked on the door and he answered without any indication that he was upset. He even helped her put a few things in her car.

She was inside when suddenly she was hit in the back of her head so hard it knocked her down. She wasn't sure what happened, or what hit her. She was confused and lays on the floor for a few seconds. The next thing she knew, he was on top of her and started to choke her. She said he used both his hands and reported he was almost sitting on her throat putting the entire weight of his body behind his hands. She states she could feel herself going unconscious. The next thing she remembered, is waking up with her wrists and feet bound by zip ties. She says she doesn't know how long she was out or how her clothes were removed. At this point, she was naked and wrapped in a sheet that even covers her head. She is being dragged through the house.

He thought she was dead. He thought that he had killed her. She cried as she said "I knew I would have to fight for my life." She described the struggle, almost getting away a few times. Screaming does her no good because there are no other houses close by. She ends up being tied to a chair naked. She reports to me that she watched him take her clothes and the sheet she was wrapped in and go into the laundry room. "I couldn't see, but it sounded like he put them in the washer."

She watched him clean up the blood with bleach and other cleaners. He tells her that she will not see the sunrise and that he knows he will eventually go to jail "So I'm going to make it worth it, but not easy for them to pin it on me." He told her that he will make sure no one finds any trace that she was even there. She reported being choked unconscious many more times in between sexual assaults.

She woke up in his bed; he was asleep next to her. She said she was so scared to move but knew that this was her chance. She was able to make it outside and to her car where she is glad to see he did not harm her two small dogs. They had been in the car since she arrived the day before. She was still naked, but jumped in and locked the doors. There was sudden panic, where are the keys? I could hear how frantic she felt as she described digging through all the items in the front passenger seat looking for them. She found them! She said she just yelled and cried out "Thank you God!" She reported fumbling trying to get the keys in the ignition before starting the car. He must have heard the car start because she reports seeing him run out the front door through the rear-view mirror as she drove away.

She tells me "I just drove home naked, like a zombie". The next thing she remembered was being in the shower. At some point, her adult daughter came in and found her sitting there under the running water. As soon as she saw her daughter's face all she could do is cry. She said that she wasn't crying because of what happened to her, she was crying because she was so afraid, she would never see her daughter again.

Her daughter drove her to the ER. The nurse I in training was shaking after documenting the victim's story. She learned how to hold the camera. I teach her that every injury needs a minimum of 3 photos. 1 picture showing the orientation of the victim so we can tell if the two following pictures are from the front or back, arm, leg, etc. The 2$^{nd}$ picture is a close-up view of the injury, and the 3$^{rd}$ has a measurement tool so that we can document the size of the injury. I could tell the nurse was holding back tears. We work methodically and slowly from head to toe. We collected as much trace evidence as we could. There were just over 100 pictures when we were done.

We also measured the circumference of her neck in two places and wrote down the measurements. This is an important step. Non-fatal strangulation is often under-treated. There is a lot of room for swelling inside the neck. Measuring helps monitor for changes and determine if the internal damage is worsening over the following few days.

We tell the officer that whoever is on the scene should look for the sheet and clothes she reported he had put in the washer. So, they could look there or in the dryer maybe? We gave him a description of the items. His response was "Do you think we should send an officer to the scene? Why?"

Um, well it's a crime scene. This was not only sexual assault; it was an ATTEMPTED MURDER! He thought he had killed her. Wait, even if it was a sexual assault, it's still a crime scene. Dude. I could watch TV and know this. I didn't have to be a forensic nurse to figure that out. How do you NOT know that?

So frustrating. I started to think about even the ER staff who checked her in. They documented the chief complaint as sexual assault, not attempted murder, assault, and strangulation. This was a big deal. Why was everyone downplaying what happened to this poor lady? She was sexually assaulted, beaten, strangled multiple times, and almost murdered!

We prepared the victim for discharge. An advocate was with her, and helped schedule follow-up visits with a doctor, get prescriptions, and arranged a safe place for the victim to go.

The other nurse and I went to the forensic office to start the long task of logging evidence and pictures. I could tell she was frazzled. As soon as the door closed, there were tears. I told her it was ok to cry. She kept asking how someone could do this to another person. All the same questions I have asked myself for years.

I do not know the outcome of this story. I don't know if he went to jail or not. I was never called to testify so I like to assume he just took a plea and there was no trial. Non-fatal strangulation is a felony in all 50 states. Hopefully, justice was served.

Just a few things people should know about strangulation:

Most victims of strangulation will have no outward signs. No bruising, no redness, no visible swelling. If there are signs the most common are: pinpoint purplish spots around the eyes or to the roof of the mouth. Many times, you might see scratches under the chin. This happens as people reach for whatever is around their neck.

The neck isn't hollow, but there is a lot of room for swelling on the inside. So, measuring as mentioned above, is key.

Strangulation is not only under treated, but under prosecuted. Studies show that those who commit non-fatal strangulation are 800 times more likely to come back later in life and kill someone. It should be prosecuted EVERY time and since it's a felony in all 50 states, I am not sure why it isn't.

# 9-year-old Male
# Grocery Store Assault

Don't let your kids use public restrooms alone

Late on a weekday afternoon, police brought in a nine-year-old boy who was at a local grocery store with his mom. He needed to go to the bathroom and his mom allowed him to go on his own as she continued shopping. He reported going into the bathroom, and standing at the urinal when an adult male already in the restroom asked him "So is it big?" The boy asked what he meant as he washed his hands.

The boy states that the man then showed him his own penis and asked "Is yours big?" He replied "I don't know" to the stranger. The man then approached the boy and unbuttoned his pants. The man pulled his pants and boxers down in the front and then "He put his whole mouth on my part". The boy states he tried to get away from the man, but the man was telling him "I'll give you money or buy you candy. Just wait for a few minutes." He said that he then told the man he had to go cause his mom was waiting outside the door.

The boy found his mom in the store and told her immediately what happened. Like most moms, she lost her mind for a minute, and then went to look for this man. Employees from the store heard the commotion and came over to see what was going on. When the mom told them what happened, the employees and other bystanders in the store hold this man there until the police arrive.

The police arrested a 25-year-old male. He admitted his crimes. I collected evidence, but there is no need for a trial as the guy took a plea. It is not very common that children are abused or assaulted by strangers, but wow, the boldness of this man.

Of course, this was not on the news either. I know they got the bad guy, but putting this stuff on blast makes people aware that these things can happen anywhere. Not just "somewhere else", not just stadium bathrooms, not just truck stops. It's everywhere.

I do have to say that while being assaulted by strangers is uncommon, traffickers are becoming more and more brazen. They are grabbing adults and kids in broad daylight from busy parking lots and grocery stores. They work in groups and don't seem to mind if they are being recorded or called out in public. They just keep going. It's terrifying.

# 3-year-old Female in CPS Custody

Our system to protect children from harm
is broken

I was called into the ER late one evening on a weekday. A 3-year-old female was brought in by Child Protective Services or CPS. The CPS caseworker explained to me that the little girl was in state custody because her mother was found guilty of physical abuse. She had been in foster care for approximately 2 months. The caseworker accompanies the little girl to weekly hour-long visits with dad at a local child advocacy center. The caseworker explains that after the visit, the little girl needed to pee. She took her to the bathroom and noted blood in the toilet and on the toilet paper as the little girl wiped herself.

She reported she knows nothing happened with dad because she was there the entire visit and never left the room. Before we get ahead of ourselves, I needed to do an exam. There can be other causes of bleeding. Let's see what the genital exam shows before jumping to conclusions.

The first thing I did, was ask the little girl questions. She didn't say a word to me. Tears roll down her cheeks silently, she did not make a sound. She wouldn't make eye contact with me. She didn't seem afraid, just so sad.

I don't know that I have ever seen a child so young sit and cry in complete silence. Not even a sniffle.

I proceeded with the exam. I always go head to toe, this way nothing is missed. Everything including her vaginal exam was normal at first. If a child has not begun puberty, we do genital exams with the patient laying in a few different positions. First, just normal laying on their back. Then we have them turn over, sit on their knees, and then put their chest down on the bed. This puts them in what is called "knee-chest position". Picture them face down with their knees underneath them and their little tush up in the air.

In the knee-chest position, I immediately recognized signs of anal penetration. She had tears in several locations around the anus. These were not initially visible due to the way the skin wrinkles because of the tightening of the sphincter. The tears were hidden within the wrinkles. I knew that these were sustained within the previous 12 hours because there was still active bleeding on some of them, and there are no signs of clotting or healing. I knew it's not been very long. This meant someone in the foster home was the perpetrator. I asked the CPS case worker who lived in the foster home. She reported that the foster parents are a married couple with 4 other foster kids, all were teenage boys. There was no way for me to know who the perp was right then and there. The evidence would have to be processed through the crime lab. Of course, all kids were removed from the home and questioned.

This poor little girl was physically abused by her mother, taken away from her family, and placed in foster care for safety where she was raped. The CPS caseworker would be responsible for informing her parents of the incident. I can't imagine that phone call.

The little girl was referred to the child advocacy center for our county. Child Advocacy Centers provide a location where CPS, Law Enforcement, Forensic Psychology, and Advocacy are all in the same place. When a psychologist is interviewing a child, the other entities involved watch in real-time from another room and in one way or another, communicate with the psychologist the questions they need answered, etc.. The interview is also recorded and can be used in court. This prevents multiple interviews and, in some cases, prevents children from having to testify in an open court.

I do not know the outcome of this case. I was never called to testify so I assume the crime lab found a DNA profile that matched someone in the foster household and that person most likely took a plea.

# 16-year-old Female
## Six Flags

**Our kids are too trusting**

This case was a tough one. I cannot imagine being a teenager in today's world. The constant connection through social media is so toxic.

16-year-old female asked to go to a party that one of the seniors from school was throwing. Her parents said no, and told her she had to stay home for the night because they were concerned about drinking at the party. She snuck out and went to the party anyway. At the party, there is a 19-year-old male whom she started talking to. She reported having a good time, no alcohol or drugs. The male was telling her how right she was and that her parents were being ridiculous. He told her that she should stay the night with him and they could just hang out for the weekend, which she was totally down for. She didn't go home the next morning either. He took her to the local mall to go shopping. She actually felt really happy. She really liked him. They were taking selfies all day and just had fun. He brought up the idea of going to Six Flags on the next day which was Sunday. It's a bit of a drive, but she was willing and thought it would be fun. At this point, she had not spoken to her parents. There are multiple texts exchanged during her mall trip back and forth between her and her mom. The guy tells her, "Maybe you should turn off your phone, so they can't track you. You can use mine, or just turn yours on here and there but not long enough for them to track it." She states she thought it was a great idea and hadn't considered the fact that they might be able to track her. She turns off her phone.

They drive through the night and are going to have to wait for Six Flags to open anyway so the guy tells her he wants to grab a room. This way they can take showers first and put all of their stuff in the room so no one breaks into his car while we are at Six Flags. Sounds reasonable, she still feels very comfortable and has been having a good time. She is still upset with her parents.

She gets to the hotel room and takes a shower and when she comes out of the shower, he handcuffs her to the bed. Immediate panic sets in. What is going on? He doesn't say anything, he just leaves the room.

She is confused. A few minutes later an unknown man enters the room. She is cuffed to the bed, naked and now she knows what is about to happen. He is the first of 7 men.

The entire day before that she spent with him at the mall shopping, laughing, having fun, and taking selfies, he was using those pictures to pimp her out on craigslist near the six flags location for the next day.

This is how easy trafficking is. Our teens are overly trusting. Obviously, it wasn't this guy's first rodeo. It was so easy for him to trick her.

The guy disappears. Police question the senior who had the party and other partygoers to see if anyone knew him. A few people had seen him around their school, but didn't really know him. He obviously is too old to be a student, so how did he get into the school? I guess really anyone can walk in and at his age, blend in or pretend to be a student.

The 7 "johns" as we call them, were not identified. To my knowledge, this case remains unsolved. Who is the 19-year-old? How many others are there?

The target population for trafficking used to be foreign populations, now it's our own American teens and young adults.

Why isn't this story on the air over and over in cities across the nation? How many teen girls might be a little more cautious if they heard this story? This should be on blast, not things like 200-year-old statues that people who weren't even born when they were created are offended by. Ugh! So frustrating!

This brings me to not another case but just sort of an FYI. This is taking place in schools across the country. Older guys purposefully befriending younger girls. They learn that girls who are new, or are eating lunch alone, or don't seem to have a lot of friends are easy targets. They befriend them. Invite them to a few school events or games. They make them feel special and like "part of the crowd". It's a trap. The girls find some hope that at least someone likes them and they feel accepted. Then something happens. The girls are drugged and a bunch of nude photos are taken, or they get them really drunk and video someone having sex with them. The girls are mortified. In the following days, these guys with pictures or videos, use them as blackmail. Moving forward they are told to tell their parents that they are in chess club or whatever event. This will explain coming home later than normal or not right after school. The girls are then pimped out TO OTHER BOYS IN THE SCHOOL or whoever else is interested. Sometimes even the "popular" females are in on it. They may be the ones to befriend someone and sort of set them up in the same manner. It's sickening.

Why is this not being talked about? Why don't we hear about this on the news? Mind-blowing, huh?

Where did our kids learn to do this? How is this happening to our kids and we don't know it? All great questions without answers.

38

# 11-year-old Female Assaulted by Biological Dad

It was her own dad

I was called into the ER late one evening. The police arrived with an 11-year-old-female who was sexually assaulted by her biological father. Apparently, her 18-year-old brother heard her crying and some sort of scuffle coming from her room. He walked in and caught dad in the act. His own dad, can you imagine what was going through the minds of the little girl and her brother? Police reported a major scuffle between dad and son. It must have been a big brawl because the little girl had blood from someone else in her hair.

I moved forward with the exam. She reported that dad had never touched her, made her feel uncomfortable, or attempted anything like this before. I collected trace evidence from her entire body, including her mouth. I can't bring myself to say why I had to collect evidence from her mouth, but something tells me if you are reading this, you most likely know why. Sickening. It was her dad!

Anyway, after the evidence is collected, it's time to discharge the little girl. I knew that I could not send her home unless dad has been arrested. I had to ensure a safe discharge. I walked over to the officer to whom I was planning to release the evidence, just to make sure, and I ask "Dad is cuffed up right?" His response "We are going to wait for the evidence and see what it shows." Excuse me!

So many thoughts race through my head. First and foremost, you don't need any trace evidence, there is an eyewitness!

I should explain that when a criminal charge is being considered, the officers call into what is known as "Intake" at the District Attorney's office. Basically, they explain the situation and then they are told to either make an immediate arrest, or file the paperwork so that a warrant can be issued later.

So, who works intake? Who are the people that are making these decisions?

These people are typically lawyers, maybe newer lawyers? I am not sure how you get this job. Maybe it's a starting point to work your way through the DA office??

The officer replies that he called intake and that was the answer he got. I asked, "Does that sound right to you?" You are forcing me to call CPS and take this poor girl from her mother and home and place her in foster care after such a horrible event.

My response was "How about you call them back and ask for a supervisor?" Boy, was he pissed. He was very offended. I tell him that I will be happy to call if he isn't up to it.

Am I crazy? The last place this poor kid should be is in CPS custody if there is another option.

After much back and forth, he calls and asks for a supervisor. He explains the situation to the supervisor and the officer was directed to make an immediate arrest. Turns out, it was the first day for the initial person that took the first call at the intake office. Shouldn't they know? I don't have a badge and I know better. How many nurses, or people in the general public, just listen to officers or intake and even if they know it's wrong, just don't say anything? Too many.

I'm not saying if you get pulled over that you shouldn't comply with the directions from a police officer. Everyone should always do that. I am saying if you are involved in any criminal case and something doesn't seem right, at least ask questions.

# 16-year-old Female Entrapment

Why? Just why?

In the early years of my ER/Forensic career, I was working in the ER one morning when a 16-year-old female was brought in by police after they discovered she had consensual sex with someone over the age of 21. Even though it was consensual, it's considered statutory rape. The victim told me she was at a local bar where she met a soldier who lived on base nearby. She reported that she was not drinking, she was not forced, she was not tricked. She consented to having sex with him. She stated she did not want to get him into trouble because that wasn't fair. When he drove her home the next morning, mom was waiting outside and not happy. The man was surprised she was only 16. Both reported never talking about age.

I collected evidence from her, treated her according to our protocol, and discharged her. The man was not only court-martialed and given jail time for statutory rape, but forced to register as a sex offender for the rest of his life.

About maybe six weeks later, I was called into the ER on my day off for a similar situation. When I enter the room, I saw the same girl.

Wait. What is going on? Another adult male had been arrested for statutory rape but the victim is the same girl from a few weeks ago?

Something isn't right. I asked her what happened and I got the exact same story. Hmmmm.

I was trying really hard to not victim blame, but I wanted to ask "Why would you go back there?" She isn't old enough to be in those bars anyway, so you know she was sneaking in. There is more than just you to think about. What about the lives of the men that end up in trouble?

I didn't ask her. I collected evidence and discharged the patient. I expressed my concerns to the detective and felt like something wasn't right but couldn't put my finger on it. Why would this girl put herself in the same position?

A few weeks later, guess what? Here she is again. Hold up. I was not moving forward without an explanation. I confront her. She knows that she is underage and what the implications are for the adult males. So, she knows the outcome for the men but continues. What gives?

She admits to doing it on purpose. She admits to sneaking into local clubs and seeking out someone to have sex with on all 3 occasions. There is no reason for anyone in these bars to consider that anyone else is under 18 years of age. Let's face it, teenagers today rarely look their age. There is no reason for a young adult male to even think about age when he is in a club for 18 and over.

Suddenly, I was overcome by anger. I was pissed at this kid. Does she not know the magnitude of what she has done? These men not only get court-martialed and jail time but are registered sex offenders for life. This impacts the rest of their lives. Jobs, relationships, etc.

The mom in me sort of took over and I laid into her. I was furious because I knew, that no matter what happens to her, the charges against the men would not change because they technically still committed the crime, even though she set them up. The detective knocked on the door. I opened it and got the "is everything ok in here?" question. UGH!

Ok, ok. Maybe it wasn't my place to jump her shit but I was pissed. I told the detective what she admitted to me. After connecting with the DA's office, they tried to charge her with false reporting but technically, what she reported was true so that didn't work. They were able to charge her with entrapment though. I am not sure what kind of time or punishment she received, but I do know it is nothing compared to the men she set up. It still makes my blood boil when I think about this case.

# Home Invasion

Most tragic home invasion case

I was called into the ER around 2 am one morning for a home invasion / sexual assault of an adult female. When I get to the ER, there are police everywhere and the room the patient is in is being guarded. This is not normal.

Most victims of crime are what we consider "No information patients". This means their names are not listed so if someone asks for them, the name just doesn't show up in the system. So, no one can mistakenly tell someone where a victim is or even that they are at the hospital.

So why are there police at the door of this patient? As I approach, I am briefed on the situation.

This victim is a married mother of 3. Her children: 16yr old female, 15yr old son, and 5yr old daughter. She has a sister that is a police officer. The patient's sister recently filed for a divorce from her husband after their 11-year-old daughter reported he was molesting her. The police officer took her daughter to make the report and a warrant was issued for the arrest of the dad.

That night the accused man went to his sister in laws house (the victim I am about to see) and was asking where her 16-year-old daughter was. On this particular night, the 16-year-old had spent the night with a friend so she wasn't home. The victim and her husband told the man to leave. He became angry and there was an altercation. The accused shot the husband and 15-year-old son in front of the mom and 5-year-old daughter. He then sexually assaulted the mom and took off.

I wasn't sure what I would find when I walked into this room. I had a victim who had just witnessed her own brother-in-law shoot and kill both her son and husband. Then was sexually assaulted by him. I also have the 5-year-old daughter in the room, and police were asking that I collect evidence from her as she is covered in blood and none of it is her own. They think the blood most likely belongs to her dad and brother, but she could potentially have blood from the perpetrator on her as well. This was a tough one. Some evidence collection takes 2-3 hours, some can take 6 hours. This was a lengthy one as the victim needed frequent breaks. She was in shock. Shortly after I completed the evidence collection, the 16-year-old daughter arrived in police protection. They went to pick her up from the friend's house she was staying with. Turns out, the perpetrator was looking for her because he didn't want her to talk. He had been molesting her for years too. During her interview, she revealed that he even made her and his daughter interact sexually so he could watch.

To my knowledge, they never found him. There were reports that he ran off to Mexico, but no one really knows.

# Smuggler Turned Trafficker

We will never catch/contain them all

Working in the ER a few hours before my shift ended, I get a call from EMS. They are transporting a female in her 50s who had been found naked and running in the streets. She doesn't speak much English so we have an interpreter in the ER who can help translate. The woman was hysterical when she arrived but I didn't understand what she is saying. The interpreter tells me that she was insisting on calling her daughter right away. I tell her ok, let me get her checked in, etc. She screamed "NOW!", so the interpreter helped her with the phone to call her daughter.

As she calms down, the patient told us that she is from Mexico and that her daughter was paying someone $5,000 to smuggle her across the border and get her to her daughter in Atlanta. She reports there were others also being smuggled. Once they crossed the border, she wasn't sure what city they were in. She states they were placed in the back of a van and taken to a house that had the windows boarded up, no furniture, and no electricity. The smuggler then pulled a gun and took all of their clothes. They were kept in that house for a few days and were given 1 bottle of water, a can of tuna, and a cookie each day. The smugglers were then communicating to the families that they were in the US but that it would now cost $8,000 if they wanted to see their loved ones again.

She tells us that they were taken to different houses, in different cities along the way, and that there were new traffickers to take over in each city. She reports being sold for sex 15 times over the last few weeks. She talked about other victims that were with them and then in some cities, those victims were taken but others were picked up. Every city they went to had a house that was set up and waiting for them.

She says they arrived in this city 2 days ago, and that today around lunchtime, the people who were holding them left. She wasn't sure how long they would be gone but as it got later, she started trying to escape. I'll never forget the way her voice sounded when she yelled in English "I got out!" She was surprised that she was able to escape. Once out of the house, she said this panic came over her as she realized they could come back at any moment and find her. She kept saying "I was naked but I just kept running from house to house." She reports knocking on several doors and that no one would open the door or help her. No one would call the police for her. Can you imagine how that felt? Being held captive, a victim of sex trafficking, and you finally escape and no one will help you. No one will open their doors or even call the police. I think to myself, what would I do if a naked woman knocked on my door in a panic screaming? I may not let her in my house, but I would at least tell her to hide on the side or in the backyard and that I would call the police. Give her a blanket, something? She reports she just kept running. Finally, she turned a corner and saw a store. She ran into the store begging for someone to call the police. The store employee called 911 and this is how she ended up in an ambulance on her way to our hospital. She was so adamant about calling her daughter right away because she wanted to make sure her daughter didn't pay the smugglers.

Within 30 minutes of her arrival, Homeland Security was in the ER to take her into protective custody. This is not uncommon. Every county has a sort of chain of command if you will, that they follow for victims of human trafficking. If it's a minor from the USA, the FBI will show up quickly. If it's a victim from another country, Homeland Security shows up.

We had to quickly clear her medically so they could take her back to try and find the house in an attempt to apprehend the smugglers and free the other victims. By the time they found it, it was cleared out and everyone was gone.

How easy it is for smugglers to turn these people into trafficking victims.

# CHRONICLES OF AN ER/FORENSIC NURSE

A few short stories from the ER that I am sure will leave you with some questions.

47

# Death Bed Confession

### The Grim Reaper

As the charge nurse in the ER of a small rural hospital, I am called to determine if a patient on the floor who is a DNR (Do not resuscitate) has passed. This is only when there are no physicians currently on the floor. This usually only happened in the middle of the night, as normally during the day, a physician is present. The protocol for this is that you listen with a stethoscope for 1 full minute, while simultaneously listening for cardiac activity and/or breathing, and also watch for the rise and fall of the chest. This was a female in her 80's who hadn't spoken or eaten in a few weeks. Basically, she was on hospice waiting to die.

Now, remember it's the middle of the night. Most lights are turned off, the hallway lights are turned down. I open the door enough that the hallway light shines into the room illuminating a pathway to the patient's bedside. I don't know why I didn't turn the light on in the room. It's not like I expect that I might wake her up, as she has been unresponsive for nearly two weeks. I walk in, get my stethoscope and lean over the bedside. I start listening and silently counting. One one-thousand, two one-thousand, etc... I get to 35 without hearing a thing, and all the sudden she takes a deep breath, and in this deep commanding voice, says "I'm alive!"

I screamed and must have jumped out of my skin. Somehow, I am airborne and moving toward the door of the room. I don't think my feet touched the ground; I am not even really sure how I got there. I know you are laughing at the mental picture you have in your head. I was laughing by the time I got to the door too, kind-of.

She scared the shit out of me! I swear I heard her giggle, so I turned around wondering, is she awake? I can't just walk out now even though I really wanted to. I walked back over to the bedside and for some reason, I apologized. I told her I was sorry, but that she scared me. I asked if she was ok and if she needed anything.

What she said to me next literally made the hair on my neck and arms stand up.

She asked, "Do you see the man in the corner without a face?" She didn't point, but somehow, I knew she meant the corner of the room BEHIND me. I wasn't about to turn around and look. I just replied "nope". She then said, "He is here for me and I know why. I am the mother of seven children and I was responsible for two of their deaths and no one ever knew it. No one will ever find their bodies."

What am I supposed to say to that? I sat there in silence for what seemed like an eternity, but I am sure was really just a few seconds. I knew this was her deathbed confession.

Looking back, my response was really dumb. I still close my eyes and shake my head when I think about what I said. I should have asked her if she had asked God to forgive her or if I could call the chaplain. Was there a family member that she wanted us to give the information to? I didn't. All I could think of was that if the Grim Reaper was in this room here to take her, I didn't want to be in there. I asked her "Is there anything I can get you? Do you want some water?".

Uhm what? I couldn't think of anything else to say, I just wanted out. She replied with a simple light whisper "no". She died later that night. When I was called a second time to pronounce her, I turned the lights on before going into the room and did not go by myself.

Am I supposed to do something with this information? It's not like there is anyone left to prosecute for the crime. If no one ever knew it, did her family not know that there were 2 kids missing? How did she do it? Why? So many questions. Oh, and is the Grim Reaper real?!

# Drugs? Crazy? Possessed?

Inhuman strength

I was the charge nurse in a pretty busy ER around lunchtime one day when police bring in a 30s-year-old male who was very combative, fighting, and had beat up his girlfriend but wasn't making any sense. He was screaming but it was like another weird language. No one could understand him. We gave him a shot of a medication that would sedate him so that he couldn't hurt anyone or himself.

Typically, in these cases, we test them for drugs and alcohol. If these things are on board, most often the patients are held in the ER until the drugs/alcohol wear off and then we release them to an adult family member. This guy had PCP in his system. He is sleeping it off for a few hours and then his girlfriend (Yes, the one he beat up) and his brother show up. By the time night shift came around, the patient was awake and calm. Normally, if drugs are onboard, we don't have the mental health team assess the mental state before they leave, but for some reason, the doctor ordered a mental health evaluation. So, I report him off to the night shift charge nurse and let her know that he will most likely be released to his girlfriend and brother once the mental health team is done.

The next morning, I arrive at work and am about to start taking report from the charge nurse to who I reported off to the night before. I happened to look up and see the PCP guy still there in the psych room. I am shocked he is still there and asked "the mental health team didn't let him go?". She replies "Oh no, we released him to his brother and girlfriend, then he went home and slit his girlfriend's throat."

Uhm what?! Did we miss something? Did he go home and do more drugs? Where was the brother? I look over at this guy who has an officer in the room. He was cuffed to the stretcher by both wrists. The side rails on the bed were up and he was holding onto them suspending himself in the air. Sort of sitting with his legs crisscrossed, and holding himself up in the air. He would remain in this position for hours, never lowering and resting on the bed at any point. He would speak in some weird dialect or I guess I don't even really know how to describe what he was saying. Was it a dialect, a different language, or was he just making sounds? I don't know, but it did seem to have a pattern to it. He later was released to police custody. By the end of the shift, the girlfriend who had been flown to a trauma hospital was out of surgery and calling to see if he was still in our hospital. What? I told her, "He just tried to kill you, why on earth would you be calling for him?" She said, "You don't understand, It's not really him. He is possessed."

Umm, I don't know what to say. Is this real? Does this really happen? I know people who believe in things like this and people who don't. If I believe in God and angels, shouldn't I also believe in hell and the devil? I feel like I've seen too much to completely discount it, but I also feel like if you don't acknowledge the negative side, then maybe it can't touch you. Is that crazy?

# Seizure or Something Else?

### Not a seizure

One day in the ER, I happened to be walking through the triage area and saw an adult male carrying a female into the door. When I say carrying, I mean they were both standing, she was facing him and he had his arms under hers, sort of walking her in. We can tell something is wrong so we grab a wheelchair and approach them. I asked what was going on and he said he didn't know, but that his wife had given birth to their baby a week before. The patient's arms are sort of contracted and stiff with her elbows bent and her hands contorted and under her chin. Both of her legs were extended and stiff. My first thought; is that she is having a seizure.

I should explain something about seizures. If you are having a true seizure, you are not conscious. You cannot respond to things around you or speak. Many people fake seizures for some reason. To tell the difference, one of the first things we do in the ER is inflict minor pain. For example, taking a pen and squeezing the pen against a fingernail, sternal rubs, etc. If the patient responds, we know it isn't a seizure. During a true seizure, I could stick a needle in your eyeball and you wouldn't flinch. Some people have what are called Focal seizures where maybe their arm twitches, but these are not unconscious full-body seizures. If you are unconscious due to a seizure, you won't respond to pain or answer questions.

I immediately think she is having a seizure because of the way her limbs are so stiff and positioned, plus, the fact that she had just given birth. There are a few conditions that can cause seizures following birth.

Because of how rigid she was, and we were in the entrance to the ER, we put her in the wheelchair but her legs are straight out and stiff. I couldn't push the wheelchair forward because her feet were pushing against the ground. So, I was pulling her backward. This was the fastest way to get her inside so we can help her. I have already tried a few things that are mildly painful to see if she responds, she didn't. About halfway to the room, she rolls her eyes up so far, you can only see the whites of her eyeballs. Then she grabbed my wrist, and started whispering

"Somebody help me, Somebody help me, Somebody help me." Over and over in rapid succession. Her voice was really creepy too. I almost stopped in my tracks. All I can think is (and I might have said out loud??) "What. The. Fuck..." We get her in the room and she starts turning her head side to side really slowly and looking at everyone with this grin. This grin and the look on her face didn't seem real. It was like her mouth was abnormally large and contorted. I don't have words to describe it but it was terrifying. We get her on the monitor, the ER staff starts doing the normal things that we do when patients come in. Her heart rate is high which is consistent with seizure activity, but she obviously is not having a seizure.

Her husband reports she hasn't been acting normal the last few days but doesn't really elaborate. CT scan of her brain is normal. EEG of brain activity does not show seizure activity. Blood work all normal. A few hours later, she is totally normal and doesn't remember anything. As the charge nurse, I help stabilize patients, keep things moving, etc.. but I don't have to stay in the room otherwise. Needless to say, I didn't spend much time in that room. No explanation that I have ever come across can explain what was happening to her or why I felt scared of her. I've had knives pulled on me outside the ER, crazy people attack me, and have been part of natural disasters. I was never scared. But I was scared of her.

# 12-year-old Female

Back from the dead

EMS calls in with 12-year-old female CPR in progress. She was found by her family in the bathtub, cold, and lifeless. The 911 operators try to have the bystanders (in this case her family) start CPR. EMS reports they arrived 6 minutes after the 911 call and that bystander CPR was poor quality.

Have you ever done CPR? It's not easy. It's a workout and most people wouldn't perform it well on a family member. You feel ribs break and it just seems brutal. It is brutal. CPR is typically pretty fast though. You try all the life-saving measures and either it works or it doesn't. Normally, this will go on for around 15-30 minutes in a hospital setting, and if it doesn't work, we call "Time of Death" and stop. Unless the patient is cold. They can be dead, but they have to be warm before you can declare them dead.

So, EMS is giving us a report of everything they have tried since they took over on scene. Total CPR from 911 call to now is 45 minutes. It is unknown how long she was lifeless in that bathtub. We take over and continue life-saving measures but add warmed IV fluids, place warming devices on the patient, etc. There was no sign of foul play, no signs of a possible suicide attempt. We aren't really sure of the cause at this time. We work her for two more hours. These are tough ones because it takes so much out of the department.

After almost 3 hours of CPR, we call Time of Death "2:38" am. I'll never forget that. She is surrounded by her family, but they can't touch her. They can't hug her or kiss her.

See, anytime someone dies in the ER, we have to call the Medical Examiner. We give them the details that we have and they decide if there is going to be an autopsy or not. Basically, was this a natural death or not? If we don't know, then they take the body for an autopsy and determine if foul play was involved or what the cause of death was. If there is going to be an autopsy, then the body is considered evidence until the Medical Examiner releases it. So, no one can touch the body until then. For children, there is always an autopsy.

This is hard. Imagine working in this situation and you try to tell the parents they can't touch her. We have an officer in the room and allow the family in the room while we are waiting for the Medical Examiner, but the officer insures no one is touching the body. I am making the necessary phone calls, etc. I am listening to the family pray over her. They are asking God "Why?" You can hear the pain without even being in the room. It is heartbreaking.

Sometimes after people die, they let out a big burst of air or something will move like an arm or leg. We often have to go back in to explain to the family that this is normal, but it doesn't mean that they are still alive. Very delicate conversations.

As I sit at the nurse's station, I am on the phone holding for the Medical Examiner and I hear the mom yell out "Praise God!" Followed by a bunch of yelling. I hand the phone to the secretary and go into the room expecting to have to explain this to the family. When I walk into the room, the officer's eyes are big and wide. He is staring at the body. As I approach the bedside, I thought I could see shallow breathing. I was thinking, "Oh, how sad. Her body is releasing the little air that is left, and it is going to give her family false hope. How do I help them understand?", but it continues. I watch carefully. There is chest rise and fall. She can't be breathing, she has been dead for now, more than 3 hours. I am so confused.

I take my stethoscope and listen for both breathing and a heartbeat. I think I actually said "HOLY SHIT" out loud. She was breathing, she had a heartbeat. I spring into action, push some buttons in the room to get some help, and start putting the monitors back on, etc. I am confused. As is the doctor and everyone else in the room that knows, this doesn't happen. How is this possible? Of course, she doesn't wake up and we put her on life support because we have no idea what's going on or why she was dead in the first place. She was dead. She WAS dead.

Holy shit. A secretary steps into the room telling me the Medical Examiner is on the phone. This is the only time in my career that I said "tell them never mind.... I think?"

The patient was flown to a hospital with a pediatric ICU. We were told that she made a full neurological recovery and was normal. No deficits, etc. What? Just What?

No explanation. Just divine intervention, and the cause of her "almost"death was never discovered.

So many questions.

# How to Become a Forensic Nurse

Every state has its own requirements and may vary but here are the basics:

> Be a Registered Nurse for at least 2 years

> Take a certification course (Most programs separate adult and pediatric training)

In many states you can look up Sexual Assault Nurse Examiner or SANE training through the Office of the Attorney General. There are also some online training options through The International Association of Forensic Nursing or Tribal Forensic programs. Established forensic programs will also provide training classes in some states.

> Train with a physician or APP for a certain number of speculum placements

As a forensic nurse, you will need to place speculums for female victims who report vaginal penetration to collect evidence. This is not something that nurses are qualified to do but can receive training for this purpose. Most states require a certain number of speculum placements with a physician / APP for training.

> Submit proof of courtroom observation. (16-20 hours of expert witness testimony)

Criminal trials are open to the public. The purpose of this is to learn how to testify as an expert witness. There are a few classes on different platforms to learn how to testify as well. The biggest tip I can give you, is that you can only testify to the evidence you collect. You cannot testify that someone was or was not sexually assaulted. What evidence did you collect and why did you collect it? That's it.

> Train with a certified forensic nurse for between 8-10 victims where evidence is collected.

This is important for obvious reasons but also because most forensic programs will have an established relationship with the local crime lab. The local crime lab will communicate what techniques or technology that they are using and have available. For example, Crime labs can establish DNA profiles from saliva faster and at a reduced cost compared to blood. Most crime labs would prefer this method and will request buccal swabs from the victim instead of blood. Where you receive your training will most likely be in the same crime lab jurisdiction and therefore, you will learn their preferred samples or techniques for submitting evidence.

In some states, you can then submit an application for certification.

Other states do not require it.

After 2 years of practice, you can then take a national certification test.

If this is something you are interested in, I encourage you to contact a local Sexual Assault Coalition, The Office of the Attorney General, or look up local Forensic or SANE programs.

# Laws of Teenage Sex;
# A few Tid- Bits for Parents

First, anyone over the age of 13 can seek medical care for their own sexual health WITHOUT parental consent. Birth control, sexual assault, STDs, etc. They can come to any ER, clinic, or doctor's office for sexual assault, pregnancy prevention, or treatment for STDs and we can treat them without notifying you. Some parents freak out about this, but it really is a good thing. If your kids aren't comfortable talking to you about it, at least they are talking to someone and taking care of themselves.

The laws of teenage sex and consent can be tricky and slightly differ per state.

All states have a "legal age of consent". This is in regard to sexual contact. In most states, it's around 16.

If both parties are under the age of 18 there is normally a clause that states their birthdays have to be within 18 months or a specific time frame of each other or the older party is liable.

It is illegal for anyone 18 and above to have sexual contact with anyone under the age of 18 even if both parties consent. This is called Statutory rape.

When it comes to texting, if a person sends a picture that is sexual in nature (not just nude photos either) .... 2 things to consider if you send the photo:

*If the person in the picture is under the age of 18, then it is considered child pornography.

*If the person receiving the picture is under the age of 18, then it is considered promoting obscenity.

If you are charged with one of these two crimes, you can be placed on the registered sex offender list.

In some states, there is a time frame that is assigned for that list. In others, once you are on the registered sex offender list, it's for life.

I was involved in a case where a 15-year-old girl's mother posted a picture on Facebook of her children in the backyard playing in the sprinklers. A boy from the 15-year-old girl's school saw it and took a screenshot. Zoomed in on the girl's chest (she had on a bikini) and he sent the picture to other boys that they all went to school with. He was charged with both child pornography and promoting obscenity. He is a registered sex offender for life.

In some cases, I feel like this list is miss used. It is there to help identify others who have a history of sexual violence/pedophiles, etc. In this case, I don't think this 15-year-old boy really meets that category but the law is a zero-tolerance law. There is no case-by-case scenario.

# CHRONICLES OF AN ER/FORENSIC NURSE

This collection barely skims the surface of what is trapped inside me. The things I cannot unsee. The evil that I know exists.

61

# The silence is deafening.

I am overwhelmed by the silence that surrounds so much violence. It is right in front of all of us, yet so many never see it.